CW00420138

WAREHAM TO SWANAGE
50 years of change

Vic Mitchell and Keith Smith

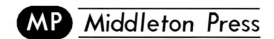
MP Middleton Press

Cover picture: A fresh station and a new signal box at Harmans Cross represent change indeed, but an SR class M7 and BR class 4 tank provide a link with past operations. The date is 23rd November 1997. (A.P.M.Wright)

Published June 2003

ISBN 1 904474 09 8

© *Middleton Press, 2003*

Design   Deborah Esher
*   David Pede*
Typesetting   Barbara Mitchell

Published by
*   Middleton Press*
*   Easebourne Lane*
*   Midhurst, West Sussex*
*   GU29 9AZ*
Tel: 01730 813169
Fax: 01730 812601

Printed & bound by Biddles Ltd,
*   Guildford and Kings Lynn*

INDEX

ACKNOWLEDGEMENTS

As press officer and official photographer to the Swanage Railway, Andrew Wright has been immensely helpful in confirming or establishing facts. We are also grateful for the assistance received from our usual helpers: G.Croughton, N.Langridge, Mr D. and Dr S.Salter and, as always, our wives.

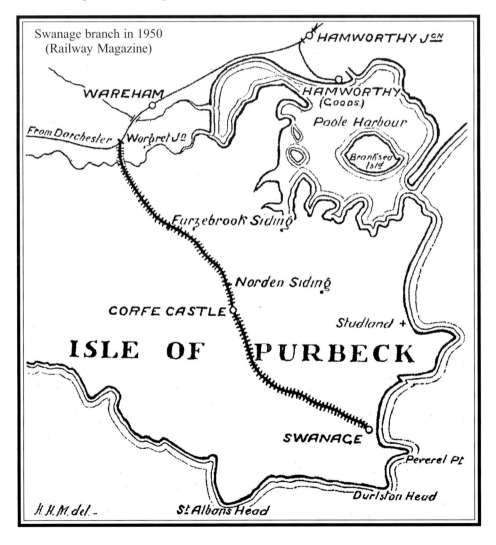

Swanage branch in 1950
(Railway Magazine)

GEOGRAPHICAL SETTING

The Isle of Purbeck is almost an island, bounded on the north by the River Frome and Poole Harbour, on the east and south by the sea, and connected to the mainland by high ground only at its western end. Its unique geology has had an important effect on railway traffic and still does. The southern area consists of Purbeck Beds, a source of good building stone; the central area yielded Purbeck marble and china clay, while the Poole Harbour shoreline is now the site of a number of substantial oil wells. The varied geology has given rise to a spectacular landscape and coastline which has attracted millions of railway passengers over the years.

The geological boundaries run east-west. The first half of the branch runs across infertile heathland before reaching Corfe Castle, situated in a gap in the impressive chalk outcrop of the Purbeck Hills. Their large angle of dip makes them a striking feature. They continue as a submarine ridge to link with the spine of the Isle of Wight at The Needles.

The route then continues on a plain of Wealden Clay to Swanage, soon running parallel to the gentle dipping stone-bearing beds to the south.

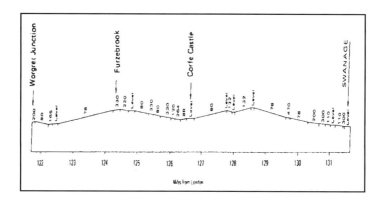

HISTORICAL BACKGROUND

London & South Western Railway trains reached Wareham on 1st June 1847 when the Southampton to Dorchester line via Ringwood came into use. The LSWR began operating the Swanage branch on 20th May 1885 and both passenger and freight traffic grew steadily.

The lines became part of the Southern Railway in 1923 and the Southern Region of British Railways upon nationalisation in 1948. The mid-1950s was the peak period for holiday traffic and a decline in local passenger traffic soon followed.

Public freight facilities were withdrawn in 1965, but clay continued to be carried from private sidings. The end of passenger service came on 3rd January 1972, but three miles of the branch were retained for mineral traffic and additional sidings were laid in 1978 to serve the Wytch Farm oilfield.

Thus 6½ miles of the branch was lifted in the Summer of 1972, but in July the Swanage Railway Society declared its intention to purchase the route. However, most of it was acquired by Dorset County Council and leased to the Swanage Railway Project from February 1975.

Rolling stock began to arrive at Swanage in 1976 and track laying began from the station in 1978. The Swanage Railway Company was formed in the following year and passengers were conveyed on 200 yards of track from 6th August 1979.

Herston Halt was created in 1984 and trains first terminated there on Good Friday. Services were extended to Harmans Cross on 4th March 1989 and the track reached Corfe Castle in 1990. However, the station could not be used until Norden was reached, owing to road traffic problems.

A large car park was constructed at Norden and train services were extended to a new station near the road to the oilfield on 12th August 1995. Two train running became possible on 12th July 1997 with the completion of the signalling at Harmans Cross.

Further track laying finally restored the integrity of the branch on 22nd August 2002 and the first train from the national network arrived at Swanage on 8th September, although regular services were a long way off.

PASSENGER SERVICES

In June 1950, the timetable showed 16 down trains on weekdays, the 4.35pm from Waterloo carrying through coaches which arrived at Swanage at 8.0pm. There were six trains on Sundays.

The Monday to Friday service in July 1955 comprised 18 branch trains, the through coaches leaving Waterloo at 10.30am. These also ran on Saturdays and there was a complete train additionally at 12.35pm, plus more through coaches on the 6.30pm. There were seven branch trains on Sundays.

In May 1960, the frequency was similar, but by June 1965 the number of weekday trains was down to 14, with the only through train originating at Bournemouth West. There were nine on Sundays, one of which started at Eastleigh.

Dieselisation in 1967 brought eleven weekday trains, two of which started at Bournemouth. There were nine on Sundays, but they ran in the Summer only, a bus being provided in the other seasons. A similar service was maintained until the end in 1972.

The service in the revival period has been precisely tailored to meet the fluctuations in visitor levels.

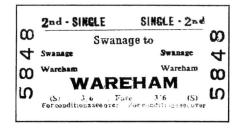

WAREHAM

1.   This is the south elevation of the impressive 1886 building. It replaced the small 1847 structure, which had been on the other side of the road. This 1965 view is little changed today. (D.Cullum)

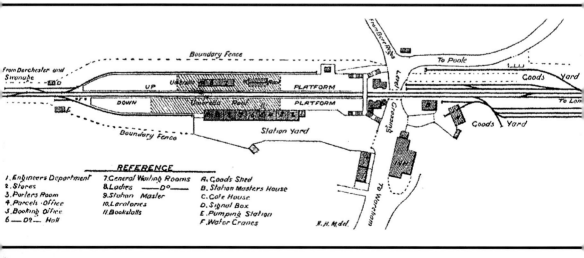

2.   The final years of steam were often spoilt by grime due to labour shortage. No. 73018 was a class 5 4-6-0 of BR design and is bound for Weymouth. This design was introduced in 1951. (Lens of Sutton)

3.   The branch train for Swanage usually departed from platform 1, having arrived at no. 4, and is seen on 20th August 1966 behind class 4 2-6-4T no. 80138. (D.Cullum)

4.   The end of regular steam on 5th September 1966 brought 3-car DEMUs of this type to the branch. No. 1128 is departing from platform 4 at 14.41 on 7th August 1969. The leading coach contains both of the 1st class compartments. (J.Scrace)

5.   This 1969 westward panorama includes the connections to both bay platforms and also the water tank, which supplied the columns at the departure end of the platforms. All have gone, as has the staff crossing. The bay tracks were lifted in 1976. (M.Turvey)

6.   The signal box was completed in 1928 and the gates in the foreground were controlled from it until 3rd April 1980, when the crossing was superseded by the bridge seen in the next picture. Seen in 1969 are tankers which were loaded here with crude oil brought by road from the Kimmeridge well. (M.Turvey)

7.   The goods yard was closed on 4th May 1970, but some sidings were retained. Electric services from London to Bournemouth began in July 1967, but the leading four coaches were devoid of motors. Known as 4TC (4 Trailer Coaches), they were detached and hauled to Weymouth. No. 33116 is propelling a 4TC set back to Bournemouth on 16th August 1981. (T.Heavyside)

8.   Another 4TC set is seen, this time on 19th September 1986. It is passing over the foot crossing, which was moved nearer the platforms and provided with colour light controls in 1987. Only 19 of the 30 levers in the signal box were in use by that time. (G.Gillham)

9.   Electric services began through the station on 16th May 1988 and were operated mainly by Wessex five-car units of this type, once an hour. This is the 12.30 from Waterloo on 5th November 1988. An additional hourly train terminated here on weekdays from 1st June 1997. (M.Turvey)

10.	History was made on 21st May 1998 when class S15 4-6-0 no. 828 *Harry A.Frith* and class M7 0-4-4T no. 30053 passed through on their way to the Swanage Railway. They had to run to Winfrith siding and then be taken by road. There had been a trailing crossover in the foreground until 1967. (A.P.M.Wright)

11.	A train of empty tankers destined for Wytch Farm has stopped at the end of the down platform for collection of a man with the key for the ground frame at Worgret Junction. The wagon behind the class 60 diesel on 7th June 1997 contains water, a recent extra safety requirement. The footbridge is unusual in having four flights of steps. (M.Turvey)

12.	A notable event recorded in other pictures in this album was the running of the first train for 30 years from the national network onto the Swanage branch on 7th September 2002. Area Signalling Manager Steve Vine is holding the single line staff and the key to the derailing block at the boundary. Coincidentally, Signalman Bob Richards had been on duty at Corfe Castle on 1st January 1972 to signal the last train *off* the branch. (A.P.M.Wright)

WORGRET JUNCTION

→

13.   The junction for the Swanage branch is over a mile west of Wareham and was controlled from the adjacent signal box until 23rd May 1976. No. 80146 is seen working the 12.30 from Swanage on 11th June 1964. (J.Scrace)

14.   The signal box steps are evident in this view of single line token transfer in the Summer of 1976. Class 33 no. D6529 is taking mostly empty wagons to the ball clay works at Furzebrook. The sheeted one probably contains other sheets. (M.Turvey)

For other views of Wareham and Worgret Junction, please see our *Bournemouth to Weymouth* album.

→

15.   The branch is in the lower left corner of this 1970 photograph of a 4TC set being propelled towards Wareham. The tall post improved signal visibility in the curved cutting. (M.Turvey)

16.   The crossover seen in picture 13 was removed following the signal box closure and trains from the branch had to run "wrong line" to Wareham subsequently. No. 47143 is about to do so with a loaded oil train on 19th August 1983 and is seen alongside the ground frame. (M.Turvey)

17.   A view from near the ground frame on 10th March 1990 features no. 47283 waiting for the catch points to move when the down line is clear. The cabinets are on the site of the signal box. (M.Turvey)

18.   The route crosses the somewhat barren landscape of Stoborough Heath, partly in cutting. Running north on 18th May 1967 with china clay wagons leading is no. 34018 *Axminster*. The end of steam was nigh and so the nameplate had already been removed. (S.C.Nash)

19.   Few passengers were to travel over the remaining three miles of the branch after 1972. "The Wessex Wanderer" contained some exceptions on Sunday 3rd April 1988. (M.Turvey)

20.   Empty tankers rattle down the branch behind no. 47376 on 8th April 1989. They will climb at 1 in 78 for 1½ miles to the sidings at Furzebrook. The oil trains ran to Llandarcy Refinery in South Wales. (M.Turvey)

FURZEBROOK

21.　　There were several firms producing china clay in the area north of Corfe Castle, but much of it was conveyed by a complex of narrow gauge railways to wharves on Poole Harbour. However, Pike Bros. also had a siding, which is shown curving away from the loop line in this 1967 photograph. (D.Cullum)

22.   Class 205 'Hampshire' DEMU no. 1127 passes over the connection to the loop, the headshunt of which is in the foreground. The 1970 picture includes the upper part of a class 33 diesel, beyond the wagons. (M.Turvey)

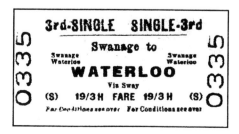

23.   A few minutes later, no. D6529 had run round the empty wagons and then shunted them onto the loaded ones. They are all being pulled out of the siding; the sheeted ones will be propelled into the loop prior to the empties being pushed into the private siding for loading. (M.Turvey)

1327 | 2nd - SINGLE   SINGLE - 2nd | 1327
Wareham to
Wareham   Wareham
Corfe Castle   Corfe Castle
CORFE CASTLE
(S)   1/8   Fare   1/8   (S)
For conditions see over   For conditions see over

24. No. 33115 is undertaking the same operation in March 1978, as work was in progress on the north side of the branch to create the Wytch Farm oil terminal. English China Clays had taken over the works in 1968 and continued to despatch by rail until 1982. (M.Turvey)

25. Clay conveyance by rail was resumed in July 1986, but using 57 ton capacity wagons of this type, instead of the traditional 10 ton design. No. 47144 is departing for Eastleigh on 10th May 1991, with wagons bound for the potteries of Stoke-on-Trent. This traffic ceased in March 1992. (G.Gillham)

26. The gate post marks the boundary of the clay loading siding and is included in picture 21. The siding had been provided when the branch opened. (V.Mitchell)

27.   By drilling deeper wells in the late 1980s, oil production was increased by a factor of about ten, far in excess of the quantity that could be conveyed by rail. Thus a pipeline was laid to Fawley Refinery, but large quantities of extra gas was produced and the railway conveyed this instead. No. 60063 is coupled to half a train on 10th September 1991; it will join this to the other half, which is in the background. The solitary wagon is in the cripple siding. (G.Gillham)

28.   Liquified petroleum gas (LPG) trains began to leave here on 20th November 1990, following the installation of new compressing and loading equipment. Almost half of every train carried butane, the remainder being propane. The methane went direct into the national gas grid. (V.Mitchell)

29.   Upon arrival, empty trains stand on the former running line, while the locomotive runs round and removes the loaded tankers from the terminal to the loop. The empties are positioned in the two sidings before departure. They are behind the fence in this 1992 view, at which time there were up to nine trains per week. By 2003, the figure was usually five. (V.Mitchell)

30.   The security gates are only open briefly during shunting operations. The loading plant is in the right background as no. 66194 returns with the "Dorset Mariner" railtour on 24th March 2001. The class 66 locomotives took over LPG trains from the class 60s. (M.Turvey)

31.   A ceremony was held on 3rd January 2002 to record the insertion of the final screw in Swanage Railway track, exactly 30 years after the branch had been closed. This is the most westerly sleeper on the private SR. (M.Turvey)

British Railways Board   (S)

CORFE CASTLE
PLATFORM TICKET 3d.
Available one hour on day of issue only
Not valid in trains.   Not transferable
To be given up when leaving the platform
For conditions see over

32.   During August 2002, the heavily overgrown half mile of track east of Furzebrook was cleared and on the 19th the stop block was removed to allow materials to be transferred from the SR to patch the disused section. (A.P.M.Wright)

33.   The reason for the sudden restoration of the link was to allow Virgin Voyager unit no. 220018 to run to Swanage for its naming ceremony. It was subject to a 5mph speed limit over the recently uncovered track. The derailing block at the boundary at Motala was unlocked on 7th September 2002 using two keys, one seen in picture 12 and the other held by SR Operations Manager, Paul McDonald - right. (A.P.M.Wright)

NORDEN

34.   About ½ mile north-west of the present station was Norden siding, which was known as Eldon's siding until 1950. (Lord Eldon owned much of the area.) The shelter spanned standard and two-foot gauge tracks. A wagon stands on the narrow gauge line on the right. This system closed in 1972, although the BR siding was taken out of use in March 1966. The signal in this August 1966 photograph is Corfe Castle down distant. (D.Cullum)

35. By 1987, the infertile trackbed had been colonised little by the plants of Norden Common. This eastward view is at the location of the future Norden station. (A.P.M.Wright)

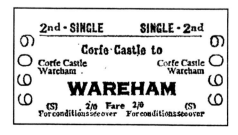

36.   An eastward panorama of the site of the new station on 20th March 1994 includes the bridge that once carried narrow gauge clay trains from the pits to the works. Another track and the platform would soon appear on the left. (M.Turvey)

37.   The new track ended close to the private road to the oilfield and the SR created the hard standing area adjacent to it to facilitate transfer of rolling stock to and from low loaders. No. D7672 *Tamworth Castle* is assisting with the loading of 4-6-2 no. 4472 *Flying Scotsman* on 20th September 1994. (M.Turvey)

38.   The station opened on 12th August 1995 and no. 34072 *257 Squadron* is seen arriving the next day. Over 20,000 people travelled in the first week. This was Britain's first Park & Ride scheme on a private railway; it resulted from successful collaboration with BP, English China Clays, Dorset County Council and Purbeck District Council. (A.P.M.Wright)

39.   After arrival, locomotives detach and run forward to the area mentioned in caption 37. No. 34072 is carrying the "Golden Arrow" symbol on 15th January 1998, the locomotive's 50th year. Historic Pullman cars were in use to recreate the prestigious continental express. The view beyond the bridge is shown in the next picture. (A.P.M.Wright)

40.   This is the site of Eldon's siding and the former clay loading dock in 1999. The black object to the right of the bridge is the chimney stack of the hut seen beside the line in picture 34. The Swanage Railway has subsequently created a siding on the right. (M.Turvey)

41.   The facilities at the station were steadily enhanced and this Southern Railway style ticket office was an early arrival. No. 80104 is one of the successful 2-6-4Ts built by BR, this example being from 1955. It is seen on 16th August 1998. (A.P.M.Wright)

42.   A waiting room shelter appeared at the Swanage end of the platform and the construction scars soon healed. Carrying its Southern Railway number, E828, the class S15 4-6-0 of 1923 has its recent nameplates showing *Harry A. Frith*. The date is 17th July 1999. (A.P.M.Wright)

43.   The Virgin special spent the night of 7th September 2002 at Eldon's siding, a name that is now back in use. The following morning, it made a dramatic approach to the station owing to the presence of a multitude of exploding fireworks. (M.Turvey)

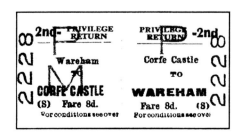

44.   The panorama from the castle includes the elegant four-arch viaduct and passing over it on 20th August 1966 with the 2.57pm from Wareham was 2-6-2T no. 41230. Steam operation ceased in September 1966. (S.C.Nash)

2nd - SINGLE   SINGLE - 2nd

9   9
5   Swanage to   5
2 Swanage   Swanago   2
   Corfe Castle   Corfe Castle
5 (s) CORFE CASTLE (s) 5
       11d. Fare 11d.

For conditions see over For conditions see over

45.   The next steam locomotive to pass over the viaduct was on 6th March 1992, when class 1F 0-6-0T no. 41708 propelled media representatives across it, as part of a publicity exercise. The track was still devoid of full ballasting. (M.Turvey)

46.   Class M7 0-4-4T no. 30053 is usually based on the Swanage Railway, but on 27th January 1993 it was leaving for a visit to the Mid-Hants Railway in connection with that line's 20th anniversary of the last BR train. That class had worked regularly to Alton. (M.Turvey)

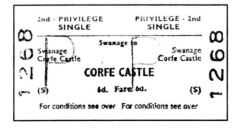

47.   Here is another case of a migrating locomotive. Ex-LMS "Jinty" 0-6-0T no. 47383 was on loan from the Severn Valley Railway, when recorded on 13th April 1996. The viaduct is listed Grade II and would have been demolished had plans for a bypass on the railway trackbed been approved. (A.P.M.Wright)

CORFE CASTLE

48.   Class M7 0-4-4Ts worked on the branch until May 1964. This example is about to depart for Wareham on 6th April 1953, but excess steam detracts from this classic castle view. (S.W.Baker)

49.   A panorama in the reverse direction shows the back of the same signal, but on 17th June 1957. Class M7 no. 30060 is working the 2.42pm from Wareham from which passengers could look down on assorted domestic architecture. The parish had a population of under 1400 at this time. (S.C.Nash)

50.   As well as a unique castle, the village had a curious signal box with unusual windows. To minimise labour requirements it was closed on 17th June 1956 and a frame was installed on the up side. The box had suffered serious settlement. (J.H.Aston)

51.   Only the rodding tunnel is evidence that a signal box had once stood between the waiting shelter and the lamp post. The passing loop was of generous length, it having been lengthened to accommodate wartime traffic. The booking office closed in 1968. (Lens of Sutton)

52.   A May 1966 photograph had the train service board blank, typical of the post-Beeching apathy. The gents had copious ventilation, the booking hall had a dormer window and the station master had four bedrooms and a bay window. (J.Scrace)

53.   The 12.40pm from Swanage on 20th August 1966 was hauled by class 4 2-6-4T no. 80019, a type that lasted to the end of steam. One of two ex-Pullman camping coaches can be seen in the goods yard. They were named *Coral* and *Milan* and were scrapped in 1968. (S.C.Nash)

54.   Within weeks prior to the end of BR Southern Region steam, the LCGB ran the "Dorset Coast Express" railtour on 7th May 1967. It was hauled down the branch by no. 34023 *Blackmore Vale* and banked at the rear by 2-6-4T no. 80011. The train is seen on its return from one of the two trips it made on the branch. The locomotive is now preserved on the Bluebell Railway as *Blackmoor Vale*. (S.C.Nash)

55. The goods yard was closed on 22nd November 1965 and coal was subsequently brought by road from Poole. DEMU no. 1105 departs for Swanage on 18th August 1967. Known as "Hampshire units", they were equally successful on this Dorset branch. (M.Turvey)

56. A lone lady waits to take her pram to Swanage on 7th March 1969, the buses not accommodating such bulky infant conveyances. In the shadow is the extension that was added in 1956 when a 12-lever frame was installed in the porters room. The smoke is from a grass fire, not the diesel engine. (G.Gillham)

57.   After almost 20 years without track, the structures were remarkably intact as restoration work began in August 1990. The building had been used by an electronics firm. (M.Turvey)

58.   Class T9 no. 120 was the first steam locomotive to pass through the station since 1967, when it reached the newly laid loop points on 10th May 1991. In its youth, the engine had been used on royal trains and its footplate was paradise for your author (V.M.) during school holidays, shunting at Hampton. (A.P.M.Wright)

LONDON to SOUTHAMPTON, BOURNEMOUTH, SWANAGE, DORCHESTER and WEYMOUTH

DOWN — MONDAYS TO FRIDAYS

		am	am	am		R am 8A20	R am	R am 8A30	R am 9A30		R am 10A30		R am 10A30	am	R am 11A30	"BOURNEMOUTH BELLE"	PP pm 12 30		R pm 12A30	R pm 1A30	R pm 1A30
LONDON Waterloo* ..dep		1 15	2❸40	5 40	Mondays only	8A20															
" Paddington ....dep																					
Southampton Central* ..arr	Via Salisbury	4❸56	7 49			10 10		10 26	11 31		11 59			1 19			1 58				3 20
Bournemouth Central* ..... "		5❸51	8 53			10 57		11 14	12 30		12 43			2 22			2 40				4 20
Bournemouth West* ..... "						11 10		11 31	12 43		1 1			2 34			2 52				4 38
Poole* .... "		6 45	9 16			11K20		11 30			12 59			3 13			3 13				4 35
Swanage* .... "	6❸48	8 40	10 9			11K58		12 19			1 54			3 59			3 59				5 21
Dorchester South* .... "	5❸28	8 18	9 53					12 7			1 32			3 58			3 58				5 15
Dorchester West .. .. "								11 55						2 50					4 17	4 57	
Weymouth* .... "	5❸42	8 38	10 7					12 9	12 22		1 45		3 2	4 18			4 18		4 33	5 14	5 33

DOWN — MONDAYS TO FRIDAYS — continued

	R pm 2A30	R pm 3A20	pm 3A30	R pm 3 30	R pm 4A20	"THE ROYAL WESSEX"	R pm 4A35	R pm 5 30	R pm 6A 0		R pm 6A20	R pm 6A30	R pm 7A30		R pm 9 0	FO pm 9 5	pm 10 30
LONDON Waterloo* ..dep																	
" Paddington ....dep																	
Southampton Central* ..arr	3 59	4 53		5 28	5 59		6 8	7 23			7 49	8 1	9 26		10❸51	11 3	12E53
Bournemouth Central* ..... "	4 40	5 40		6 26	6 47		6 55	8 26			8 34	8 41	10 13				2 14
Bournemouth West* ..... "	4 53	5 57		6 40	6 59		7 13	8 39			8 46	9 1	10 27				
Poole* .... "	5 16	6 0		7 3			7 10					8 58	11F23				2 35
Swanage* .... "	6 0	6 49					7 52					9 42					
Dorchester South* .... "		6 47					7 42					9 30	11C34				3 18
Dorchester West .. .. "			6 44						9 54								
Weymouth* .... "		7 5	6 57				7 55		10 8			9 43	11C51				

Left-hand marginal notes: "Fridays only 15th July to 24th August"; "Fridays only"; "Except Fridays 24th June to 9th September"; "24th June to 9th Sept."

DOWN — SATURDAYS ONLY

	am 1Z15	am 2❸40	am 5A40	am 7A 0	am		am	R am 7A30	R am 7A52	am 7 57	R am 8A15	R am 8630	am	R am 8A45	am	B am 9A15 9624
LONDON Waterloo* ..dep	1Z15	2❸40	5A40	7A 0			7 5			7 57						
Southampton Central* ..arr	4❸56	7 49	8 33				9 10	9 30	9 40	9 51	10 10	10 28	10 50	10 51	11 0	
Bournemouth Central* ..... "	5❸51	8 53	9 35					10 18	10 28	10 38	10 50				11 58	
Bournemouth West* ..... "							10 32		10 50							
Poole* .... "	6 45	9 21					10 43		11 22		11 33				12 17	
Swanage* .... "	6❸48	8 40	10 9	9 59			11N22	11 22	11 24						12 32	
Dorchester South* .... "	5❸28	8 18	9 59				10 48									
Dorchester West .. .. "					11 23			11 33		11 49					12 54	
Weymouth* .... "	5❸42	8 38	10 13		11 38		11 1								1 8	

DOWN — SATURDAYS ONLY — continued

	R am 9A35	am 9A30	am 9A35	R am 9A42	am 10 5		R am 10 30	am 10A54	R am 11A 5	R am 11 22	R am 11A30	am	am 11 35		R pm 12 20
LONDON Waterloo* ..dep	9A35	9A30	9A35	9A42	10 5		10 30	10A54	11A 5	11 22	11A30		11 35		12 20
Southampton Central* ..arr	11 16	11 31	11 31	11 42			11 59	12 23	12 44	12 55	1 20		1 11		2 6
Bournemouth Central* ..... "	12 18	12 30	12 43	12 37			12 46		1 40	1 53	2 26	2 16			2 51
Bournemouth West* ..... "	12 30								1 54	2 11	2 38				3 4
Poole* .... "	12 52						1 3			2 9	2N55				
Swanage* .... "							2L10	2 10		3 4					
Dorchester South* .... "			1 10				1 35			2 41					
Dorchester West .. .. "															
Weymouth* .... "			1 27				1 55			2 54					

Column marginal notes across Saturdays sections: "2nd July to 20th August"; "Until 25th June and again commencing 27th August"; "2nd July to 27th August"; "Until 3rd September"; "16th July to 6th August"; "Until 10th September"; "Until 10th September"; "Until 10th September"; "2nd July to 27th August"; "Until 10th September"; "17th September only"; "Until 10th September"

A	Seats may be reserved at a fee of 1/- per seat, upon personal or postal request to the Station Master. Early application is advisable	F	Arr 10 55 pm 25th July to 26th August	PP	1st and 3rd Class Pullman Cars only between Waterloo, Southampton Central and Bournemouth. For supplementary fees and further information, see page 44
B	Refreshment Car provided until 10th September	FO	Fridays only		
C	25th July to 26th August	G	Seats may be reserved for Poole and beyond only, see note "A"		
D	Southampton Docks Station	H	Until 10th September	R	Refreshment Car for whole or part of the journey
E	Southampton Terminus Station	K	4th July to 5th September	Z	Dep 1 25 am until 27th August
		L	On 17th September only	❸	Third Class only
		N	2nd, 9th July and 13th, 20th, 27th August only		

PP ... see page 44

LONDON to SOUTHAMPTON, BOURNEMOUTH, SWANAGE, DORCHESTER and WEYMOUTH—continued

DOWN — SATURDAYS ONLY—continued

LONDON	BOURNEMOUTH BELLE"	PP pm	R pm	R pm	25th June to 27th Aug.	pm		R pm	R pm	R pm	Until 10th September	pm	17th September only	pm	Until 10th September	pm	R pm
„ Waterloo* .. ..dep		12 30	..	12A35		12 54	..	1 22	1A30			2630		2A30		2A34	3 20
„ Paddington ......dep		..	12A30	..		..		..	..	1A35		..		..		..	.. 3A30
Southampton Central* ..arr		1 58	..	2 12		2 30		2 59	3 20	..		4 3		4 3		4 8	4 53
Bournemouth Central* .... „		2 40	..	3 0		3 33		4 0	4 20	..		4 46		4 46		4 54	5 40 ..
Bournemouth West* .. .. „		2 52	..	..		..		..	4 38	..		..		..		5 4	5 58 ..
Poole* .... „		..	..	3 15		..		..	4 35	..		5 8		5 8		5 18	6 0 ..
Swanage* .... „		..	..	3 59		..		..	5 21	..		..		..		6 0	6 49 ..
Dorchester South* .... „		..	..	3 50		..		..	5 15	..		5 40		5 40		..	6 47 ..
Dorchester West .. .. „		..	4 19	..		..		..	..	5 5		..		..		..	.. 6 44
Weymouth* .... „		..	4 35	4 3		..		..	5 33	5 20		5 57		5 57		..	7 6 6 57

DOWN — SATURDAYS ONLY—continued

LONDON	R pm	R pm	"THE ROYAL WESSEX"	R pm	R pm	Not on 2nd, 16th, 23rd, 30th July and 6th August	pm	R pm	2nd, 16th, 23rd, 30th July and 6th August only	pm	R pm	R pm	R pm		pm	pm	❸ am
„ Waterloo* .. ..dep	3 30	4A20		4A35	5 30		6A 0			6A 0			6A30	7A30	..	9 5	10 30 ..
„ Paddington ......dep	..	..		..	..		..			..			..	..		am	..
Southampton Central* ..arr	5 26	5 59		6 8	7 23		..			..			8 1	9 26		11 3	12E53 ..
Bournemouth Central* .... „	6 26	6 47		6 55	8 26		..			..			8 41	10 13		..	2 14 ..
Bournemouth West* .. .. „	6 40	6 59		7 13	8 39		..			..			9 1	10 27		..	.. ..
Poole* .... „	7 3	..		7 10	..		..			..			8 58	10 55		..	2 35 ..
Swanage* .... „	..	..		7 52	..		..			..			9 42	..		..	.. ..
Dorchester South* .... „	..	..		7 42	..		..			..			9 30	11 34		..	3 18 ..
Dorchester West .. .. „	..	..		..	..		9 54			10 2			..	..		..	.. 4‡15
Weymouth* .... „	..	..		7 55	..		10 8			10 23			9 43	11 51		..	4 30 ..

DOWN — SUNDAYS

LONDON	am	R am	R am	R am	R am	R am	BOURNEMOUTH BELLE"	PP pm		R pm		pm
„ Waterloo* .. ..dep	3❸25	8A30	9A30	10A30	..	11A30		12 30	..	1A30	..	2 54
„ Paddington ......dep	..	..	..	..	11A 0	..		..		..		..
Southampton Central* ..arr	5❸39	10 33	11 26	12 3	1 17	..		1 58		3 11		5 24
Bournemouth Central* .... „	6❸18	11 26	12 23	12 45	2 17	..		2 40		4 12		6 34
Bournemouth West* .. .. „	..	11 44	12 36	1 4	2 29	..		2 52		4 24		..
Poole* .... „	8 29	11 44	..	1 6	3 5	..		3 5		4 36		..
Swanage* .... „	11 13	12 27	..	1 57	3 54	..		..		5 22		..
Dorchester South* .... „	11 11	12 20	..	1 51	3 50	..		3 50		5 19		..
Dorchester West .. .. „	..	..	..	..	..	3 19		..		..		..
Weymouth* .... „	11 28	12 34	..	2 4	3 35	4 7		4 7		5 36		..

DOWN — SUNDAYS—continued

LONDON	R pm	R pm	R pm	R pm	R pm	pm
„ Waterloo* ..dep	..	4A30	6A20	6A30	8 30	10 30
„ Paddington ......dep	3A30	..	..	..	..	am
Southampton Central* ..arr	..	6 4	7 48	8 23	10 22	12E53
Bournemouth Central* .... „	..	6 50	8 44	9 24	11 3	2 14
Bournemouth West* .. .. „	..	7 2	9 3	9 43	11 14	..
Poole* .... „	..	..	9 6	9 46	..	2 35
Swanage* .... „	..	..	..	..	..	..
Dorchester South* .... „	..	..	9 47	10 33	..	3 18
Dorchester West .. .. „	7 25	..	..	..	..	..
Weymouth* .... „	7 40	..	10 0	10 47	..	3 34

Summer 1955

———————→

59. This is the busy scene during Easter of 1992, when great efforts were made to complete the up platform line and the long siding. However, the SR was prevented from using the station as a terminus until Norden station and car park had been built. (M.Turvey)

60. The serious limitations of the roads in Corfe necessitated restriction of access to the station and train service extension to Norden was necessary instead. This December 1993 photograph was taken after all the parking spaces had been allocated to local residents by the district council. (M.Turvey)

———————→

61. Volunteers attended to every detail to faithfully recreate the 1956 signalling arrangements. Levers out of use are painted white. (M.Turvey)

62.   This is Corfe Castle on the first day of operation to Norden, 12th August 1995, when crowds were able to alight to enjoy the high standard of station restoration. The M7 had been equally well renovated after repatriation from a museum in the USA in 1987. (A.P.M.Wright)

63.   Two photographs from 1st December 1996 show part of the pre-Christmas operation, during which time about 9500 passengers were carried. This is more than the population of Swanage. (A.P.M.Wright)

64.   At the other end of the coaches was USA-designed 0-6-0T no. 30075, rescued from Yugoslavia. The train shuttled from Swanage, all other stations being closed. (A.P.M.Wright)

65.   Boat trains had been consigned to history in Dorset since the demise of the Weymouth service, until the "Waverley Boat Train" ran on 22nd September 1996. The connecting vessel is seen in the last photograph in this album. (A.P.M.Wright)

66.   The memorable special train shown in picture 54 was re-staged 30 years later, using the original headboard, but not the original locomotive; that was many miles away on the Bluebell Railway. However, the sky was reported to be equally threatening. (A.P.M.Wright)

67.   The goods shed was put to a new use as a railway museum and the van at the dock was adapted to serve as a cinema and exhibition coach. The station has been impeccably restored, while successfully creating additional features for visitors. (A.P.M.Wright)

NEAR CORFE CASTLE

68.   The route has carried a variety of types of locomotive and train over 50 years. Recorded on 23rd August 1958 was empty compartment stock hauled by 700 class no. 30695 and M7 class no. 30108. Both classes were introduced in 1897. The train is north of Corfe Castle and is travelling towards Wareham. (S.C.Nash)

69.   Trackbed preparation near the A351 Afflington Bridge, south of Corfe Castle, was recorded on 8th April 1990. Much labour was also required to renovate drains and cesses, a topic often overlooked by passengers. (M.Turvey)

70.   The third photograph in this trilogy takes us to the Virgin Voyager visit of 8th September 2002. It arrived carrying guests and ran public trips during the day. (A.P.M.Wright)

HARMANS CROSS

71. This 1966 eastward view towards Swanage has the community of Harmans Cross on the left, the dwellings being mostly on the A351. The station was built on the other side of the bridge from which this picture was taken. (D.Cullum)

72. Work on the new station and loop was progressing well when recorded on 7th May 1988. The matting prevents clay penetrating the ballast. (M.Turvey)

73. A photograph from 3rd September 1988 reveals further progress and completion of the loop. The leaning tool van is on the site of points that would serve two sidings. (M.Turvey)

74.	The opening took place on 4th March 1989, giving a three-mile run from Swanage. The locomotives are ex-LMS no. 47383 and ex-MR no. 41708 and they are hauling a special train of six coaches containing SR Premier Life members on 3rd December 1988. Harman's Cross was the first wholly new railway station to be built in Dorset for over half a century. (A.P.M.Wright)

75.	The loop line catch point is evident as ex-GWR 0-6-0PT no. 7752 arrived on 16th September 1989 with its smokebox door red hot. The engine was from the Birmingham Railway Museum and was one of five locomotives in steam for the Steam Gala Weekend. (M.Turvey)

76.　　Class T9 4-4-0 no. 120 runs round its train on 25th April 1992 and is about to pass over the facing point lock. This locomotive is part of the national collection. (M.J.Stretton)

77. Future plans envisaged a passing loop here. The LSWR-style signal box is seen nearing completion on 10th June 1995, as class M7 no. 30053 passes over the siding points. Passing of trains here became possible from 12th July 1997. (M.Turvey)

78. The SR excels at staging special events and a vintage transport rally on 12-13 September 1998 produced over 100 vehicles and more than 2000 visitors. The 1927 class S15 no. E828 is heading towards Swanage and is pictured with a slightly younger Austin 7. (A.P.M.Wright)

79. During the same event, class 1F ex-Midland Railway no. 41708 of 1880 operated an impressive goods train. Most of the population will have never witnessed the commotion of loose coupled wagons. (A.P.M.Wright)

────────────►

80.   The SR recognises the increasing interest in diesel preservation and offers special weekends for students of modern traction. Recently named *Stan Symes*, no. 33012 in red undercoat, runs passed the operational signal box on 28th November 1999. (M.Turvey)

81.   The box interior was completed to the same high standard as the exterior. The frame had controlled electric trains for most of its life at Gunnersbury. The box can be seen in pictures 80 and 81 in our *Willesden Junction to Richmond* album. (A.P.M.Wright)

────────────►

82.   Some out of season services are operated by DMUs, such as this class 108 unit which carries the "Purbeck Line" logo. It is waiting to leave for Swanage on 23rd September 2000, while further station enhancement is taking place. (M.Turvey)

83.	The waiting shelter is seen incomplete in the previous picture and is here adorned with bunting for its official opening on 7th September 2002. The Southern Railway image extends to the target-style name sign. (A.P.M.Wright)

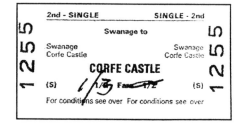

HERSTON HALT

84.   The loop was incompletely ballasted, but the platform was nearing completion when photographed on 23rd October 1983. Until opened on Good Friday 1984, trains simply ran to the stream bridge by the engine shed at Swanage. (M.Turvey)

85.   Hawthorn Leslie 0-4-0ST no. 3931 of 1938 arrives on 5th April 1988. It had propelled its train to a point half a mile west of the halt to give passengers a return trip of three miles. The high standard of coach restoration is always to be seen. (T.Heavyside)

86.   Two visiting locomotives were recorded on 20th May 1990. Ex-GWR 0-6-2T no. 5619 stands in the loop, as ex-GER 0-6-2T no. 69621 runs into the platform. It is not normally possible to pass two passenger trains here, but special dispensation was given by the Railways Inspectorate for the weekend. (M.Turvey)

2nd · SINGLE

Swanage To

CORFE CASTLE

5d. FARE 5d.

FOR CONDITIONS SEE OVER

7848 CHILD (S)

CHILD (S) 7848

87.   When imported, the Vulcan-built 0-6-0T was given a number that followed those used by the Southern Railway for this type. It is passing stock stored in the loop on 18th August 1993. (T.Heavyside)

88.   A rare crowd arrived on 12th June 1999 in connection with the unveiling of a stone (centre left) to commemorate the 15 year association of the Royal Corps of Signals with the Swanage Railway. Soldiers and volunteers have done splendid work together. (A.P.M.Wright)

SWANAGE
(Pre-closure)

89.   At busy times in the 1950s, through trains to and from Waterloo used the main platform, while local trains were confined to the shorter bay platform. One such push-pull service is headed by class M7 no. 30111. (Lens of Sutton)

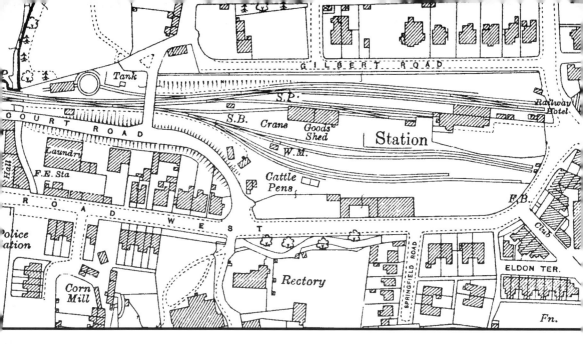

Although published in 1928, this map shows a layout that remained unchanged until the 1960s. The scale is 25 ins to 1 mile.

90.   A BR class 4 2-6-4T is signalled for the main platform in the Summer of 1964. The turntable is obscured by a large mound of ash. (C.Phillips)

91.   Seen nearer the platform is BR class 4 2-6-0 no. 76011 with through coaches from the Midlands via the Somerset & Dorset line. Their crimson lake livery made a change from Southern green that predominated in earlier years. (C.Phillips)

92.   A panorama from the bridge on 12th June 1964 includes the home signals and 2-6-4T no. 80164 with two coaches and a van from Wareham. Note that direct access to the shed across the turntable was not possible. (J.Scrace)

93.   The goods yard closed to traffic on 4th October 1965, but some sidings continued to be used for coach storage, as recorded on 1st February 1966. The small building left of centre had been built as an air raid shelter, while the one on the right served as the weighbridge office. (D.Cullum)

94.   The leading compartment was devoid of seats and used for bicycles and/or mailbags in many "Hampshire" units. No. 1102 was photographed on 7th March 1969 on the single line, all connections to which had been rendered redundant on 6th June 1967 and removed soon after, along with the turntable. (G.Gillham)

95.   The station had been extensively modernised in 1938, but gas lighting was retained. No. 1102 is seen later the same day and is serving another lady with a perambulator, by then often shortened to pram. (G.Gillham)

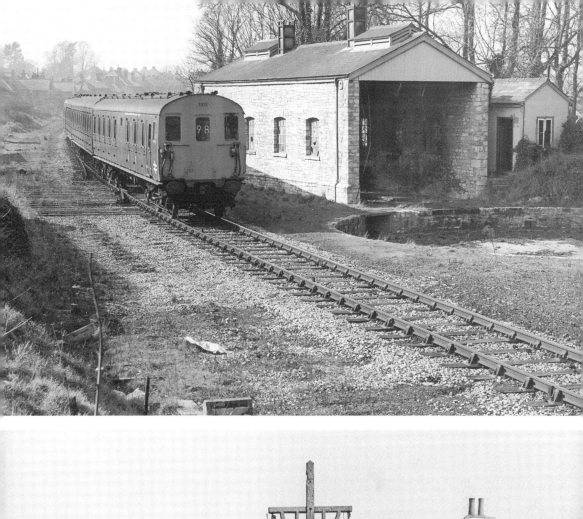

96.   No. 1128 had just worked the 13.13 service from Wareham on 23rd August 1969, peak holiday season; but no longer were there through trains serving the Midlands, but there was still one train to and from London. (J.Bird)

SWANAGE
(Closure)

97. The basic railway stood abandoned for a short time before being lifted, but fortunately all the stone structures remained. The Swanage Railway Project was soon active, despite the daunting prospects. No. D6580 hauled the final BR train collecting material on 23rd June 1972 and track lifting was completed in early September. (J.Kellaway)

98. Even the engine shed remained intact. The land became the property of the local authorities and the area from here eastwards was leased to the SRP in 1975. (J.Kellaway)

SWANAGE
(Post-closure)

99.   A symbolic length of track was soon laid to raise morale, and rolling stock began to arrive in 1976. The site had to be cleared of vast amounts of rubbish. (J.Kellaway)

100.   This hand operated GWR crane helped reduce the labour requirements and made track laying a little easier. A small petrol powered 0-4-0 arrived in June 1976. (J.Kellaway)

101.   Passengers were carried over a short distance from 6th August 1979, hauled by 0-4-0ST *Richard Trevithick*. Seen on 27th August 1981 is 0-4-0ST *Cunarder* running towards two coaches in the platform. While much track had been relaid, most of the yard had been lost. Work on the run-round loop started in 1982. (M.Turvey)

102.   Outside the shed on 3rd April 1988 was
ex-BR diesel no. 08476, in the company of ex-
MR 0-6-0T no. 41708 from the Midland Railway
Centre. In the shed is class B4 0-4-0T *Normandy*,
on loan from the Bluebell Railway. The
replacement turntable had come from London
Transport at Neasden. (M.Turvey)

103.   *Normandy* is seen in close up, having been
turned and placed alongside the original coaling
stage. The crane reduced the amount of coal
shovelling until replaced by an elevator.
(M.Turvey)

104.   Facing down Station Road on 5th April 1988 were two appealing locomotives appealing for
funds for restoration. Few in this busy shopping street could be unaware of the railway. An earlier
local poll resulted in 83% of residents supporting its full restoration. (T.Heavyside)

105.   Working trains on 12th November 1989 was ex-GWR 0-6-0PT no. 7752. Nearby is a former SR "Brighton Belle" motor coach, which had Pullman 3rd class accommodation. It had been particularly useful during the period of propelling trains here. (V.Mitchell)

106.   Heavy rain early on 3rd February 1990, combined with a high tide, isolated Swanage by road and created problems for the railway, and not for the first time. The river is covered over in the town centre and thus has limited flow capacity here. (M.Turvey)

107.   The Heritage Railway Association top national award for excellence was awarded to the SR in 1997 and was presented in January 1998. Retained for one year, the trophy comprises the coat of arms used on LBSCR locomotives when hauling Queen Victoria's royal train. (A.P.M.Wright)

108.   Among the varied events staged by the SR was the launch of the 100th book from Middleton Press, *Branch Lines to Exmouth*. Proprietors, Vic and Barbara Mitchell (left) are with Keith Smith outside the line's excellent bookshop on 25th April 1992. Funds generated from book sales please all concerned. (A.P.M.Wright)

109.   Preservation history was made when two unrebuilt Bulleid "Pacifics" departed together on 19th March 1993. Leading is no. 34105 *Swanage* from the Mid-Hants Railway and following is the line's resident "Spam Can", no. 34072 *257 Squadron*. (M.Turvey)

110.   Pullman coaches stand behind no. D3591 on 3rd September 1995, as the much loved old favourite M7 no. 30053 accelerates its train. Note that cars have taken the place of loco parts; repairs were by that time undertaken at the nearby Herston Works, which is not rail connected. (P.G.Barnes)

111. No. 34072 *257 Squadron* is seen from a fresh viewpoint on 6th April 1996. From here we can glimpse the coal elevator and also the water tank. Ex-LMS 0-6-0T no. 47383 started its working life in East London in 1927 and was on a two-month visit from the Severn Valley Railway. (A.P.M.Wright)

112. Pullman cars stand in the bay platform, which came back into use on 22nd May 1995. With its train clear of the crossover, no. 30075 is ready to start on 27th April 1996. It was built to an American design in 1960 in Croatia and purchased in Slovenia in 1990. (A.P.M.Wright)

113. Excavation for the foundations of a new signal box began in wet weather in January 1999, but the ground began to slip. Large rocks were used as a first aid measure until sheet piling could be undertaken. (M.Turvey)

114. A crowded locomotive depot was recorded on 19th October 1999 with the visiting N7 nearest, BR class 4 2-6-4T no. 80104 next and sister no. 80078 beyond. The ash wagon is squeezed onto the shortest siding on the line. (M.Turvey)

115. An elegant locomotive stands beside an impressive embryonic signal box on 25th March 2000. No. 80078 is in the process of running round and the box will eventually control a revised layout, intended to facilitate through running to Wareham. (M.Turvey)

———————▶

116. The 40-lever frame had been made in 1935 for Brockenhurst "B" Box, where it served until October 1978. The renovated equipment came into use on 6th January 2003, having justly received a National Railway Heritage Award in the previous month. (A.P.M.Wright)

117.   Few visitors would realise that locomotives are turned by manpower out of their sight. The driver of 2-6-2T no. 41312 takes a breather while others sweat in September 2001. The engine weighs over 70 tons. (A.P.M.Wright)

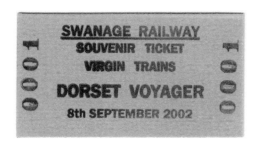

SWANAGE RAILWAY
SOUVENIR TICKET
VIRGIN TRAINS
DORSET VOYAGER
8th SEPTEMBER 2002

118.   Many thousands crowded the area as Virgin Voyager no. 220018 arrived for its naming ceremony on 8th September 2002. The curtains on the right initially covered the *Dorset Voyager* nameplate. The trains were a victim of their own success and insufficient were built to maintain an adequate service resulting in a frequency reduction being planned for 12 months later. (A.P.M. Wright)

119.   A photograph from 1st April 2003 features the station house, which the SR uses as offices. The bus obscures the booking hall, beyond which are rooms leased by a taxi firm. Buses link the station with Bournemouth and travel direct on the Sandbanks Ferry, usually hourly. (A.P.M.Wright)

120.   An alternative means of reaching the railway on 3rd September 1995 was by the steam powered *PS Waverley*, which was built for the LNER in 1946. The remains of the coal pier is in the foreground. For boat times telephone 0845 130 4647 and for trains ring 01929 425800. (P.G.Barnes)

Middleton Press

Easebourne Lane, Midhurst, W Sussex. GU29 9AZ Tel: 01730 813169 Fax: 01730 812601
Email: enquiries@middletonpress.fsnet.co.uk   *If books are not available from your
local transport stockist, order direct with cheque, Visa or Mastercard, post free UK.*

BRANCH LINES
Branch Line to Allhallows
Branch Line to Alton
Branch Lines around Ascot
Branch Lines to Ashburton
Branch Lines around Bodmin
Branch Line to Bude
Branch Lines around Canterbury
Branch Lines around Chard & Yeovil
Branch Line to Cheddar
Branch Lines around Cromer
Branch Line to the Derwent Valley
Branch Line to East Grinstead
Branch Lines of East London
Branch Lines to Effingham Junction
Branch Lines around Exmouth
Branch Lines to Falmouth, Helston & St. Ives
Branch Line to Fairford
Branch Lines around Gosport
Branch Line to Hayling
Branch Lines to Henley, Windsor & Marlow
Branch Line to Hawkhurst
Branch Lines around Huntingdon
Branch Line to Ilfracombe
Branch Line to Kingsbridge
Branch Line to Kingswear
Branch Line to Lambourn
Branch Lines to Launceston & Princetown
Branch Lines to Longmoor
Branch Line to Looe
Branch Line to Lyme Regis
Branch Line to Lynton
Branch Lines around March
Branch Lines around Midhurst
Branch Line to Minehead
Branch Line to Moretonhampstead
Branch Lines to Newport (IOW)
Branch Lines to Newquay
Branch Lines around North Woolwich
Branch Line to Padstow
Branch Lines around Plymouth
Branch Lines to Princes Risborough
Branch Lines to Seaton and Sidmouth
Branch Lines around Sheerness
Branch Line to Shrewsbury
Branch Line to Swanage *updated*
Branch Line to Tenterden
Branch Lines around Tiverton
Branch Lines to Torrington
Branch Lines to Tunbridge Wells
Branch Line to Upwell
Branch Lines of West London
Branch Lines around Weymouth
Branch Lines around Wimborne
Branch Lines around Wisbech

NARROW GAUGE
Branch Line to Lynton
Branch Lines around Portmadoc 1923-46
Branch Lines around Porthmadog 1954-94
Branch Line to Southwold
Douglas to Port Erin
Douglas to Peel
Kent Narrow Gauge
Northern France Narrow Gauge
Romneyrail
Southern France Narrow Gauge
Sussex Narrow Gauge
Surrey Narrow Gauge

Swiss Narrow Gauge
Two-Foot Gauge Survivors
Vivarais Narrow Gauge

SOUTH COAST RAILWAYS
Ashford to Dover
Bournemouth to Weymouth
Brighton to Worthing
Eastbourne to Hastings
Hastings to Ashford
Portsmouth to Southampton
Ryde to Ventnor
Southampton to Bournemouth

SOUTHERN MAIN LINES
Basingstoke to Salisbury
Bromley South to Rochester
Crawley to Littlehampton
Dartford to Sittingbourne
East Croydon to Three Bridges
Epsom to Horsham
Exeter to Barnstaple
Exeter to Tavistock
Faversham to Dover
London Bridge to East Croydon
Orpington to Tonbridge
Tonbridge to Hastings
Salisbury to Yeovil
Sittingbourne to Ramsgate
Swanley to Ashford
Tavistock to Plymouth
Three Bridges to Brighton
Victoria to Bromley South
Victoria to East Croydon
Waterloo to Windsor
Waterloo to Woking
Woking to Portsmouth
Woking to Southampton
Yeovil to Exeter

EASTERN MAIN LINES
Barking to Southend
Ely to Kings Lynn
Ely to Norwich
Fenchurch Street to Barking
Hitchin to Peterborough
Ilford to Shenfield
Ipswich to Saxmundham
Liverpool Street to Ilford
Saxmundham to Yarmouth
Tilbury Loop

WESTERN MAIN LINES
Bristol to Taunton
Didcot to Banbury
Didcot to Swindon
Ealing to Slough
Exeter to Newton Abbot
Newton Abbot to Plymouth
Newbury to Westbury
Paddington to Ealing
Paddington to Princes Risborough
Plymouth to St. Austell
Princes Risborough to Banbury
Reading to Didcot
Slough to Newbury
St. Austell to Penzance
Swindon to Bristol
Taunton to Exeter
Westbury to Taunton

MIDLAND MAIN LINES
St. Albans to Bedford
Euston to Harrow & Wealdstone
St. Pancras to St. Albans

COUNTRY RAILWAY ROUTES
Abergavenny to Merthyr
Andover to Southampton
Bath to Evercreech Junction
Bath Green Park to Bristol
Burnham to Evercreech Junction
Cheltenham to Andover
Croydon to East Grinstead
Didcot to Winchester
East Kent Light Railway
Fareham to Salisbury
Frome to Bristol
Guildford to Redhill
Reading to Basingstoke
Reading to Guildford
Redhill to Ashford
Salisbury to Westbury
Stratford upon Avon to Cheltenham
Strood to Paddock Wood
Taunton to Barnstaple
Wenford Bridge to Fowey
Westbury to Bath
Woking to Alton
Yeovil to Dorchester

GREAT RAILWAY ERAS
Ashford from Steam to Eurostar
Clapham Junction 50 years of change
Festiniog in the Fifties
Festiniog in the Sixties
Festiniog 50 years of enterprise
Isle of Wight Lines 50 years of change
Railways to Victory 1944-46
Return to Blaenau 1970-82
SECR Centenary album
Talyllyn 50 years of change
Wareham to Swanage
Yeovil 50 years of change

LONDON SUBURBAN RAILWAYS
Caterham and Tattenham Corner
Charing Cross to Dartford
Clapham Jn. to Beckenham Jn.
Crystal Palace (HL) & Catford Loop
East London Line
Finsbury Park to Alexandra Palace
Holbourn Viaduct to Lewisham
Kingston and Hounslow Loops
Lewisham to Dartford
Lines around Wimbledon
Liverpool Street to Chingford
London Bridge to Addiscombe
Mitcham Junction Lines
North London Line
South London Line
West Croydon to Epsom
West London Line
Willesden Junction to Richmond
Wimbledon to Beckenham
Wimbledon to Epsom

STEAMING THROUGH
Steaming through Cornwall
Steaming through the Isle of Wight
Steaming through Kent
Steaming through West Hants

TRAMWAY CLASSICS
Aldgate & Stepney Tramways
Barnet & Finchley Tramways
Bath Tramways
Brighton's Tramways
Bristol's Tramways
Burton & Ashby Tramways
Camberwell & W.Norwood Tramways
Clapham & Streatham Tramways
Croydon's Tramways
Dover's Tramways
East Ham & West Ham Tramways
Edgware and Willesden Tramways
Eltham & Woolwich Tramways
Embankment & Waterloo Tramways
Exeter & Taunton Tramways
Greenwich & Dartford Tramways
Hammersmith & Hounslow Tramways
Hampstead & Highgate Tramways
Hastings Tramways
Holborn & Finsbury Tramways
Ilford & Barking Tramways
Kingston & Wimbledon Tramways
Lewisham & Catford Tramways
Liverpool Tramways 1. Eastern Routes
Liverpool Tramways 2. Southern Routes
Liverpool Tramways 3. Northern Routes
Maidstone & Chatham Tramways
Margate to Ramsgate
North Kent Tramways
Norwich Tramways
Reading Tramways
Seaton & Eastbourne Tramways
Shepherds Bush & Uxbridge Tramways
Southend-on-sea Tramways
Southwark & Deptford Tramways
Stamford Hill Tramways
Twickenham & Kingston Tramways
Victoria & Lambeth Tramways
Waltham Cross & Edmonton Tramways
Walthamstow & Leyton Tramways
Wandsworth & Battersea Tramways

TROLLEYBUS CLASSICS
Croydon Trolleybuses
Derby Trolleybuses
Hastings Trolleybuses
Huddersfield Trolleybuses
Maidstone Trolleybuses
Portsmouth Trolleybuses
Reading Trolleybuses
Woolwich & Dartford Trolleybuses

WATERWAY ALBUMS
Kent and East Sussex Waterways
London to Portsmouth Waterway
West Sussex Waterways

MILITARY BOOKS
Battle over Portsmouth
Battle over Sussex 1940
Blitz over Sussex 1941-42
Bombers over Sussex 1943-45
Bognor at War
Military Defence of West Sussex
Military Signals from the South Coast
Secret Sussex Resistance
Surrey Home Guard

OTHER RAILWAY BOOKS
Index to all Middleton Press stations
Industrial Railways of the South-East
South Eastern & Chatham Railways
London Chatham & Dover Railway
London Termini - Past and Proposed
War on the Line (SR 1939-45)

BIOGRAPHY
Garraway Father & Son